S&OP Jumpstart!

A Primer for Implementation and Improvement

Eric J. Tinker

Pace Publishing Company

ISBN: 978-0-9969088-3-2

Pace Publishing Company

Contents

All companies need S&OP

The challenges in today's global environment make business tougher all the time.

- Uncertainty and variability
- Complexity
- The pressure to implement new technologies
- Not enough staff or resources
- Political unrest, natural disasters, pandemic
- The pressure to just deliver more

If your team isn't functioning like a proactive, well-oiled, machine that makes coordinated decisions in the best interest of the whole that produce results, the leader(s) won't be there too long. I've seen the pressures on my clients only get larger over the years. They need all the tools they can get.

S&OP defined.

> **S&OP is management's vehicle for planning, communication, performance management, and intermediate-term decision making across functions to produce business results.**

All companies need S&OP

S&OP is a linking process.

S&OP sits below corporate strategy and above the functional planning processes. I often find that companies have a strategy and can execute the day-to-day with varying degrees of efficiency, but it's this middle layer of intermediate-term planning that is often missing or ineffective. I like to say that S&OP "operationalizes" the strategy.

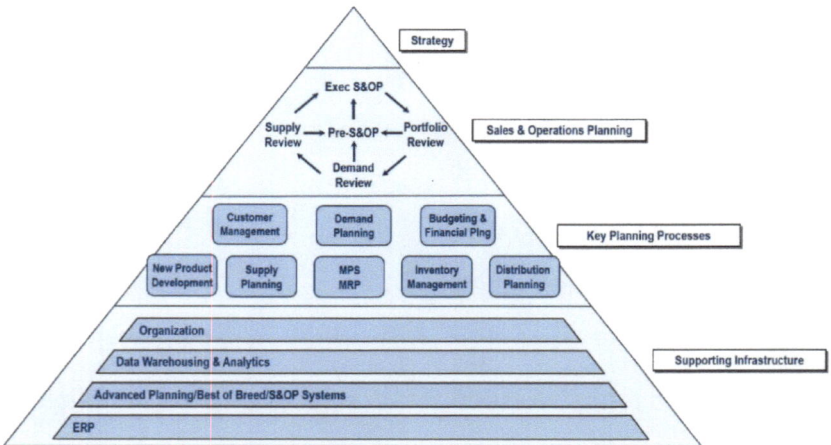

S&OP is an aggregate level discussion (e.g. product family/brand, business unit, enterprise), it's not in the weeds of SKUs and individual orders. There's some infrastructure to it as well. We'll discuss more about these things.

All companies need S&OP

Characteristics and benefits include:

- A structured, repeatable, collaborative framework that defines accountability for underlying processes and results

- Led by senior management

- Exception-based discussions

- Consistent plans used throughout the organization

- Management of financial gaps while there is still time to do something about it

- Alignment of discussion and decisions across functions in accordance with the strategic direction of the company

- Business performance management across the enterprise

- Platform for continuous improvement in the company

- Leadership development and improved teamwork in the company

All companies need S&OP

The most common functions with the largest roles in S&OP include:

- Sales
- Marketing
- Demand Planning
- Operations and Supply Chain (including areas such as manufacturing, planning, inventory management, procurement, distribution)
- New Product Development/Portfolio Management
- Finance

The exact design and involved functions depend upon your value chain. While S&OP may have started in manufacturing, it has now expanded beyond that in recent years to very different value chains. Nexview has a few experiences here.

When you ask which companies or industries need S&OP? You can also ask which companies need to forecast their business, align resources to meet demand for goods and/or services, and then translate that operating plan into a set of financials.

Sounds like every company to me.

Key design elements

The "typical" S&OP flow

In the most basic and tangible sense, S&OP is a set of meetings. While each design and the terminology used needs to be matched to the needs of the business, there is a best practice baseline design that has evolved in manufacturing companies.

This is a continuous process which I why I draw the cycle as shown on the next page. While there's a linear sequence within any one monthly cycle, the teams are continually working their areas, including preparing for the next cycle when their part in the current one finishes. I also draw Pre-S&OP in the middle because it is the hub that links everything else.

Other important parameters to determine are:

- The planning horizon (no. of rolling months in the future the process will cover)
- The frequency of the meetings (usually monthly)
- The S&OP calendar – The week of the month each S&OP component (meeting) takes place, see the table at the end of this section for a typical calendar
- The frozen period or time fence for planning

Key design elements

S&OP is a continuous cycle.

Executive S&OP
- Address items escalated from Pre-S&OP
- Confirm the S&OP Plan
- Regional and/or BU roll-up
- Review of Executive KPI Scorecard

Pre-S&OP
- Rolling plan comes together
- Exceptions resolved across functions
- Involve only those who are required
- Resolve majority of issues in Pre-S&OP rather than in Executive S&OP

Supply Review
- Evaluate ability to meet unconstrained demand
- Confirm the Supply Plan
- Confirm inventory position
- Review KPI Scorecard

Portfolio Review
- Exception based review of new product introductions and supply chain implications
- Evaluate longer-term product opportunities in context of the portfolio
- Review KPI Scorecard

Demand Review
- Critically review forecast
- Challenge ourselves to fill gaps
- Consensus Unconstrained Demand
- Review Demand related KPIs

The basic components aren't the full design.

S&OP designs need to be integrated with the organization design and the way the company financially reports. Furthermore, the data underlying structure needs to support the required views and roll-up/down reporting. For larger organizations (e.g. multiple business units, regions, plant sites) this can often require some discussion and may also lead to discussion about the structure of the company.

Key design elements

The S&OP design should align across these 3 legs.

Answers to further design questions integrate the process.

- How many different meetings of each type should we have?

- How does the rolling period needed for S&OP integrate with the budgeting horizon?

- Do we need regional/BU level S&OP's first, then roll those up to a corporate/global one?

I discuss these things, more on best practices, and process maturity characteristics in my other publications, all of which are beyond the intended scope of this brief primer. Please see the next chart for a summary of the S&OP components.

Key design elements

Summary of S&OP components

Item	Portfolio Review(s)	Demand Review(s)	Supply Review(s)	Pre-S&OP(s)	Executive S&OP
Typical Timing	Week 1	Week 1	Week 2	Week 3	Week 4
Objectives	■ New products ■ Discontinuances ■ Profitability ■ Promotions ■ Manage budget & KPIs	■ Confirm Demand Plan ■ Manage budget & KPIs ■ Identify issues	■ Confirm Supply Plan ■ Identify constraints & issues ■ Manage budget & KPIs	■ Confirm Operating Plan ■ Resolve cross-functional issues ■ Manage budget & KPIs	■ Confirm Operating Plan (enterprise view) ■ Resolve executive cross-functional issues ■ Strategic decisions ■ Manage budget & KPIs
Owner and Facilitator	■ VP Marketing ■ Product Mgmt	■ VP Sales ■ Demand Mgr(s)	■ VP Operations ■ Supply Planner	■ S&OP Sponsor ■ Director of SC	■ CEO/GM ■ S&OP Sponsor
Outputs	■ New product demand ■ Info for supply chain	■ Confirmed unconstrained Demand Plan ■ Issues for Pre-S&OP	■ Confirmed Supply Plan ■ Issues for Pre-S&OP	■ Confirmed Operating Plan ■ Decisions ■ Issues for Executive S&OP	■ Confirmed Operating Plan (enterprise view) ■ Decisions
Participants	■ Marketing ■ Demand Mgmt ■ Finance	■ Sales ■ Demand Mgmt ■ Finance	■ Supply Mgmt ■ Operations ■ Procurement ■ Finance	■ Directors and Managers	■ Management Team

Roles & responsibilities

Roles and responsibilities need specific definition.

This means written out and shared during training. We often use the common RACI chart approach.

The sponsor is the key role.

In S&OP, the most important role is the overall sponsor. If the sponsor isn't at least a Vice President, you won't have a true S&OP process. If the sponsorship isn't at the right level, the important decisions for the company will be made outside of the process and S&OP will be used for tactical execution coordination (e.g. orders, SKUs). While the latter is still necessary, it just isn't S&OP. A sponsor needs to:

- Allocate resources and ensure executive participation
- Provide guidance
- Communicate the vision, be visible, and accountable
- Ensure the key decisions are made through the process
- Demand results

Roles & responsibilities

The sponsor can come from any part of the organization as long as s/he has enough background and cross-functional influence.

Most sponsors are either P&L owners or Vice Presidents of Supply Chain. The component meetings also have sponsors. These are the functional VPs and owners of the underlying processes and plans who also participate in the Executive S&OP meeting.

Finance is now an integral part.

Finance is an integral part of each meeting and needs to keep the focus on the budget, monetize volume plans, integrate S&OP with the budgeting process, and help with business cases for scenarios to support decision making.

Roles & responsibilities

Summary of roles & responsibilities

Executive Sponsor

- Sponsors the Executive S&OP Meeting
- Communicates the Vision and ensures use of the process at the executive level
- Uses the process to manage / prepare for corporate and board interactions
- Resource allocation
- Demands results

S&OP Lead

- Leads and integrates the entire process
- Develops agendas for Pre-S&OP and Executive S&OP
- Change management and consensus building at all levels
- Broad subject matter knowledge
- Up and coming executive

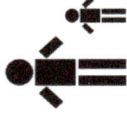

Component Meeting Sponsor

- Member of the executive team
- Executive leader for this area, owns the plan, and KPI performance
- Represents function at Executive S&OP
- Resource allocation for their area
- Makes decisions and demands results

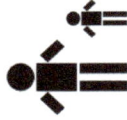

Component Meeting Facilitator

- Lead for functional area and leads meeting
- Ensures plan/report preparation and maintains for area of responsibility
- Integrates issues across functions
- Represents function at Pre-S&OP

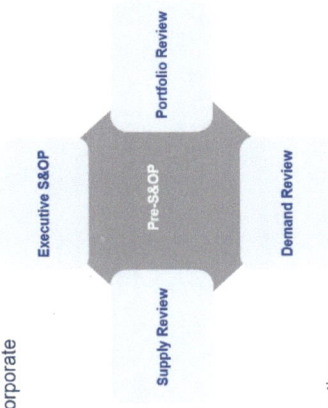

Meeting Sponsor

Meeting Facilitator

Executive S&OP

Portfolio Review

Pre-S&OP

Demand Review

Supply Review

Use a proven approach

If you haven't been through this before, you may be wondering what the big deal is. Isn't this just a few meetings? Yes, it's meetings, but also reports/plans and KPIs that are all linked and layered. It fits with the org design and integrates with an executive management system above, and the tactical processes and execution below. Pretty easy to understand what the meetings are as described in preceding figures, but it gets more complicated beyond that. Many implementations are sub-optimal or just fail.

Keep these tips in mind for implementation:

- Conduct general training to start, followed by training specific to your design and process during rollout

- Pilot with a receptive area of the business

- Integrate your rollout with your IT capability

- Start the executive meeting in month ~3 of the rollout

- Measure financial results

- Get it 60 – 80% right during launch, then improve

- Meetings will take approximately 3 cycles to become productive

- Communication, project, and change management

Use a proven approach

Nexview's methodology has been proven over several implementations.

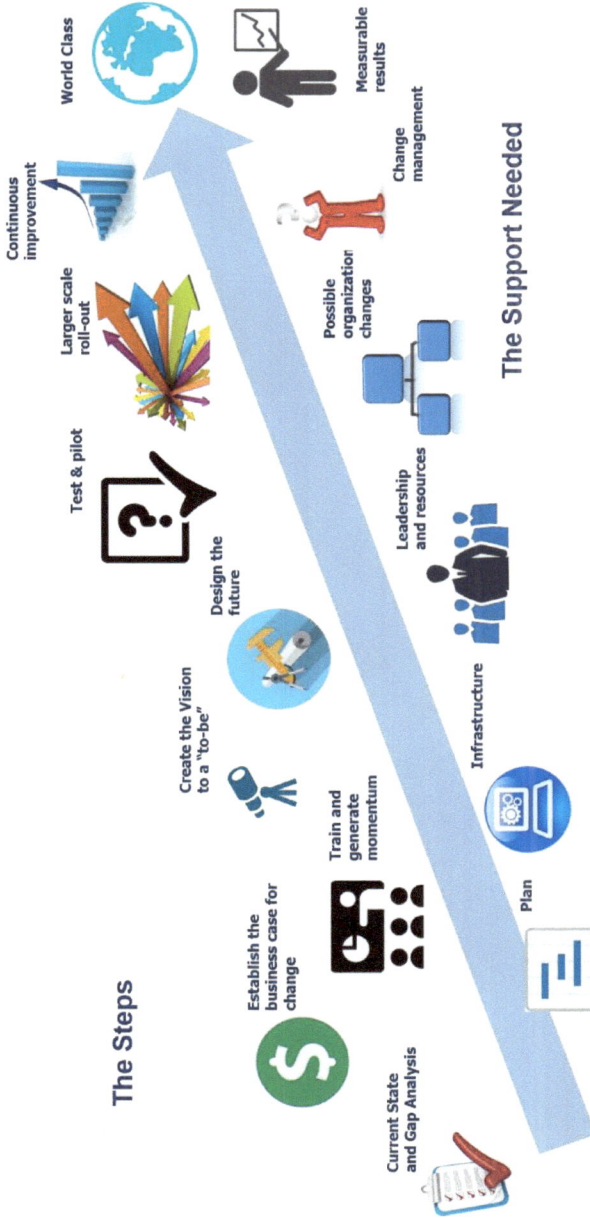

The Steps

- Current State and Gap Analysis
- Establish the business case for change
- Train and generate momentum
- Create the Vision to a "to-be"
- Design the future
- Test & pilot
- Larger scale roll-out
- Continuous improvement
- World Class
- Measurable results

The Support Needed

- Plan
- Infrastructure
- Leadership and resources
- Possible organization changes
- Change management

Of-course the approach isn't cookie-cutter, we adapt it each time, but these overall steps are usually required.

Use a proven approach

Project duration is dependent upon your size, complexity, benefit commitment, and degree of change management required.

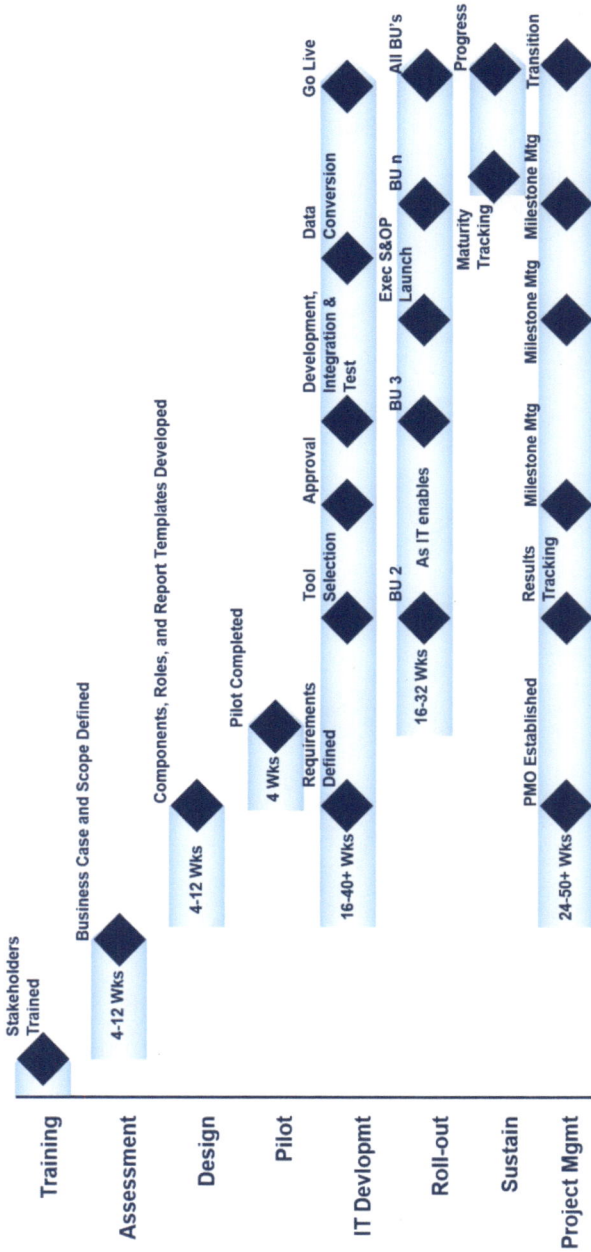

Training
- Stakeholders Trained

Assessment
- 4-12 Wks
- Business Case and Scope Defined

Design
- 4-12 Wks
- Components, Roles, and Report Templates Developed

Pilot
- 4 Wks
- Pilot Completed

IT Devlopmt — 16-40+ Wks
- Requirements Defined
- Tool Selection
- Approval
- Development, Integration & Test
- Data Conversion
- Go Live

Roll-out — 16-32 Wks
- BU 2
- BU 3
- As IT enables
- Exec S&OP Launch
- BU n
- All BU's

Sustain
- Results Tracking
- Maturity Tracking
- Milestone Mtg
- Milestone Mtg
- Milestone Mtg
- Progress

Project Mgmt — 24-50+ Wks
- PMO Established
- Milestone Mtg
- Transition

IT is required to enable S&OP

While S&OP is a people process, it is also data intensive. Each meeting has its own emphasis/cut of the overall plan and there's an underlying data structure/hierarchy. There's also KPI reporting in each meeting. IT must be involved and considered during the design phase or it could sink the ship during implementation.

Basic IT requirements

- Data that people trust
- Report at any level in the product and business hierarchy
- Report history and plans over a rolling planning horizon
- Highlight exceptions and create charts from base reports
- Monetize currency plans
- Make changes at higher levels in the product hierarchy and cascade those to the SKU level
- KPI reporting

IT is required to enable S&OP

We categorize IT as follows:

Spreadsheets

- Used by over 80% of our client base and survey respondents in some way. I'd say this is okay for a pilot, but spreadsheets alone will limit your ability to scale and sustain.

ERP and Data Warehouse with Reporting Tools

- Provides base historical data, but most of S&OP is about the future which will be predicted some other way.

Supply Chain Planning Tools

- Provides predictive capability and scenario modeling. Systems are becoming cheaper and easier to implement. If you're serious about improvement, the path leads here at some point.

IT has a maturity path too.

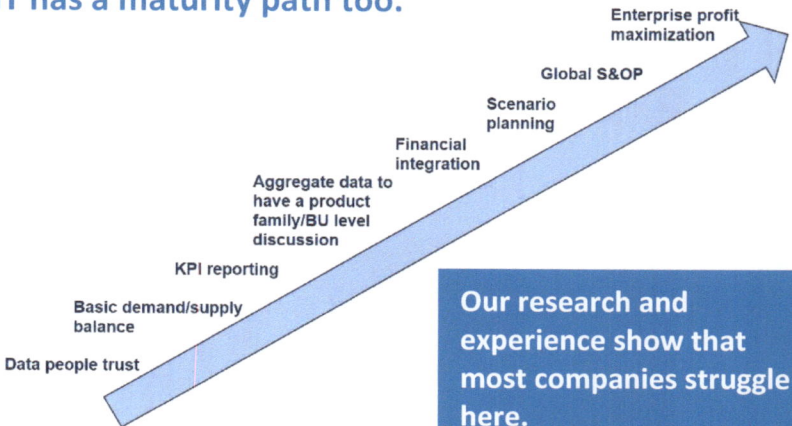

Enterprise profit maximization

Global S&OP

Scenario planning

Financial integration

Aggregate data to have a product family/BU level discussion

KPI reporting

Basic demand/supply balance

Data people trust

Our research and experience show that most companies struggle here.

IT is required to enable S&OP

Some systems are using advanced technologies.

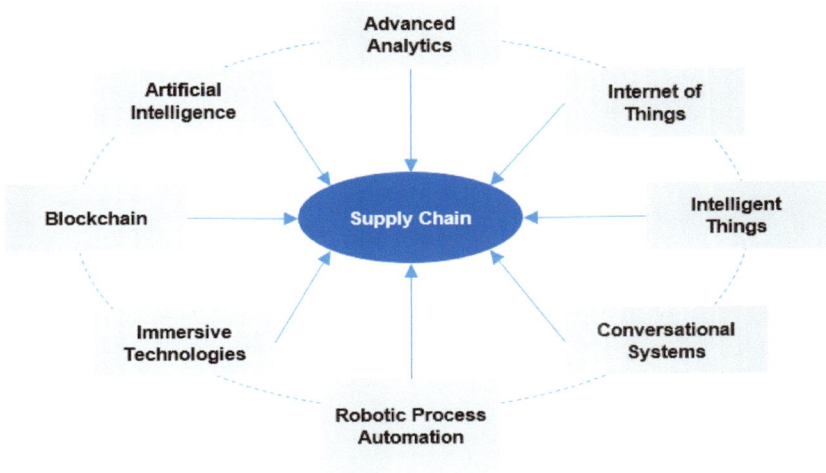

The relevant technologies primarily gather data and analyze tactical data to help establish trends, correlations, and other inputs to help support longer-term S&OP-level decisions.

> **If you are not working on applications for these technologies, you are falling behind.**

8 levers for performance

We have found that focusing on these 8 levers during design or revitalizing efforts will help the team be successful.

I've discussed some of these topics already, so I'll focus on a few of the others here, and address Results and Change Management in later sections.

Vision

A vision for S&OP describes the characteristics of the end state. For this application, I suggest it's more tactical and specific than what a vision for a company might be. We always establish a vision right away with the project team and we come up with 8-12 tight bullet points around scope, what we

8 levers for performance

will achieve by when, how we'll use S&OP, some intangibles, and also some quantifiable results. In cases where there is inadequate sponsorship, or little/no assessment, teams usually struggle with putting a number on a KPI as part of the vision. If this is the case, it's a gap.

Organizational alignment

This one intersects with some of the others. I'll emphasize:

- Your S&OP design needs to be integrated with the organization structure.
- The vision is used to communicate, educate, set expectations and common goals, manage scope, and evaluate success.
- Results measurement and change management techniques are integral to aligning the organization, more on this later.

Reports and tools go with the meetings.

S&OP meetings have items that go with them to guide the conversation, support decision making, and keep things on track.

8 levels for performance

Several things go with the meetings to make them impact the business.

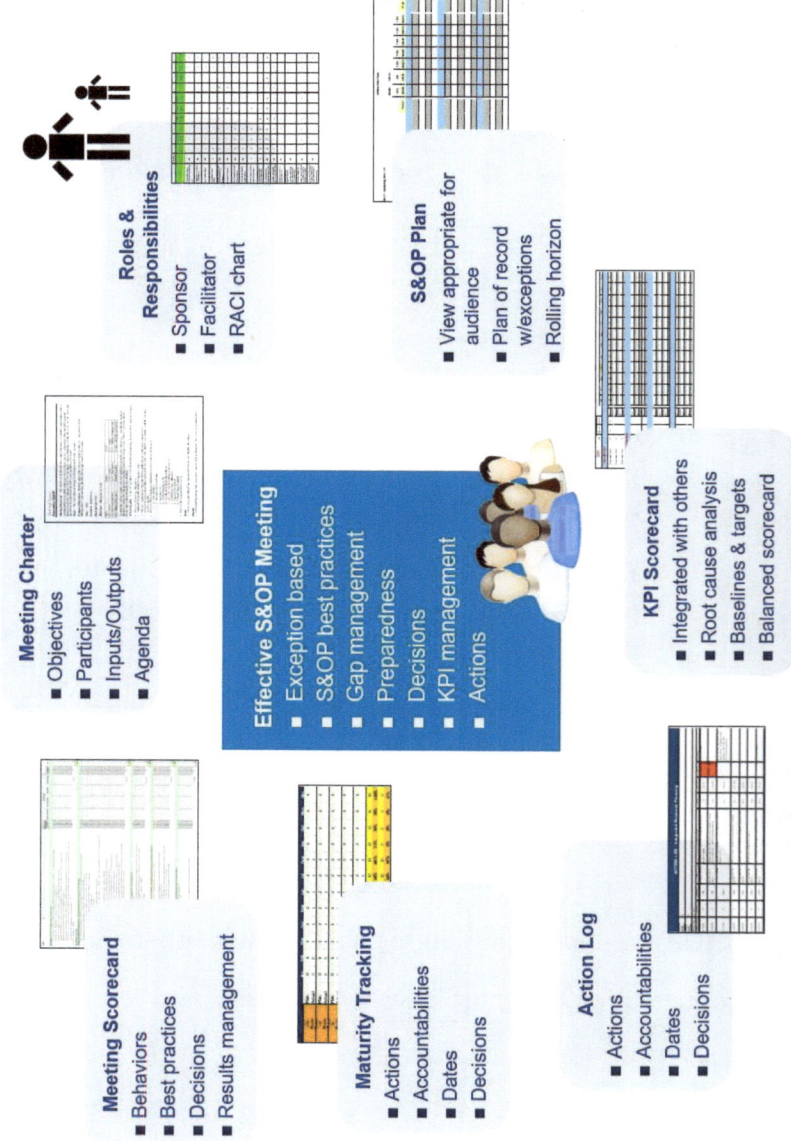

Roles & Responsibilities
- Sponsor
- Facilitator
- RACI chart

S&OP Plan
- View appropriate for audience
- Plan of record w/exceptions
- Rolling horizon

Meeting Charter
- Objectives
- Participants
- Inputs/Outputs
- Agenda

Effective S&OP Meeting
- Exception based
- S&OP best practices
- Gap management
- Preparedness
- Decisions
- KPI management
- Actions

KPI Scorecard
- Integrated with others
- Root cause analysis
- Baselines & targets
- Balanced scorecard

Meeting Scorecard
- Behaviors
- Best practices
- Decisions
- Results management

Maturity Tracking
- Actions
- Accountabilities
- Dates
- Decisions

Action Log
- Actions
- Accountabilities
- Dates
- Decisions

8 levers for performance

S&OP plans show aggregate quantities in monthly buckets over the planning horizon.

The idea is that the overall operating plan of a company builds up in the early meetings of the cycle, with each accountable function focusing on their part of the overall plan (e.g. the Commercial group confirming a Demand Plan in Demand Review, and same on the supply side). The plans come together in the later meetings (Pre-S&OP and Executive S&OP) to show a consolidated view of quantities that vary with each other. It's a design topic, but typical quantities shown are:

- Sales, Production, Inventory for Make-to-Stock situations
- Orders, Production, Backlog for Make-to-Order situations
- If you have both MTO and MTS, the solution becomes a point for the design discussion

Companies need both volume and currency versions of the plans. Quantities are shown and discussed at product family/brand levels then roll-up from there to business unit and company (e.g. for Executive S&OP).

Results are necessary for success

Why are we doing S&OP? It's a good idea? It helps us communicate better? It helps us work as a team? All good reasons, but what are those things for? To get results.

S&OP is too hard and too much work to not get anything quantifiable out of it. A lack of results, or the lack of diligence to track and show them are typical reasons why S&OP processes fail or get reduced to the tactical. No results? Any naysayers in the stakeholder population will either be all over that, or just check out.

We normally recommend an assessment.

Many want to just jump into this before an aligning assessment is completed. Others do something cursory that produces a loose benefits case that no one will sign their name to. We tailor the level of assessments to client situations (and budgets), but after doing this for 20+ years, what we do is probably very different from client led efforts. You'll need your business case when the project gets challenging and you ask someone in a high place to do something differently, or when the next shiny object to chase comes up. It's usually 3-4 months into the project.

Results are necessary for success

Key steps in an assessment are:

Get input from Stakeholders

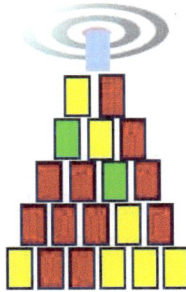

Assess as-is processes/capabilities relative to best practices and determine gaps

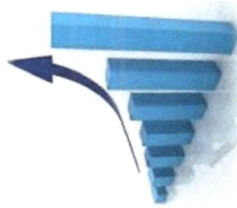

Complete quantitative studies on potential improvement areas

You can do the assessment upfront to align stakeholders around gaps and a business case, or later when you need to justify the project in the face of a challenge that pops-up.

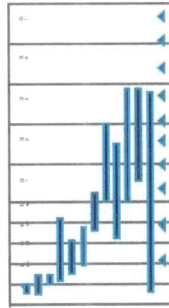

Quantify and time improvement opportunities

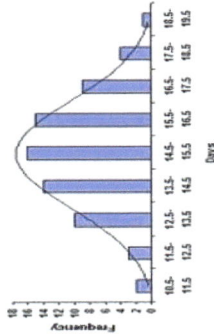

Define and scope the project based on the assessment

Results are necessary for success

Recall that S&OP is an over-arching, planning, coordinating, and decision-making process.

It does produce results in time, but with so many variables in business, the naysayer could also say the results were due to something else. S&OP channels human energy to produce results. The results can come by working at this higher level, or by working in the underlying processes and tactical areas to drive improvement faster. We recommend both. I wrote my first book, *S&OP Results – Find, Measure, and Manage Results Throughout Your Supply Chain* about this. Note that "Supply Chain" is in the title too.

KPIs are a good place to start.

We advocate completing an assessment that produces a benefits case, then structuring a project around that to get defined benefits over a defined period of time. That's a large undertaking and while there's an ROI, some companies (especially in the mid-market) aren't up for that. They want improvement, but sometimes don't want to commit resources and time for an assessment phase. Whatever the situation, every company needs to at least baseline and start measuring KPIs or the effort will degenerate to just a good idea.

Results are necessary for success

KPIs need to be integrated, linking upward to the executive balanced scorecard and downward to execution.

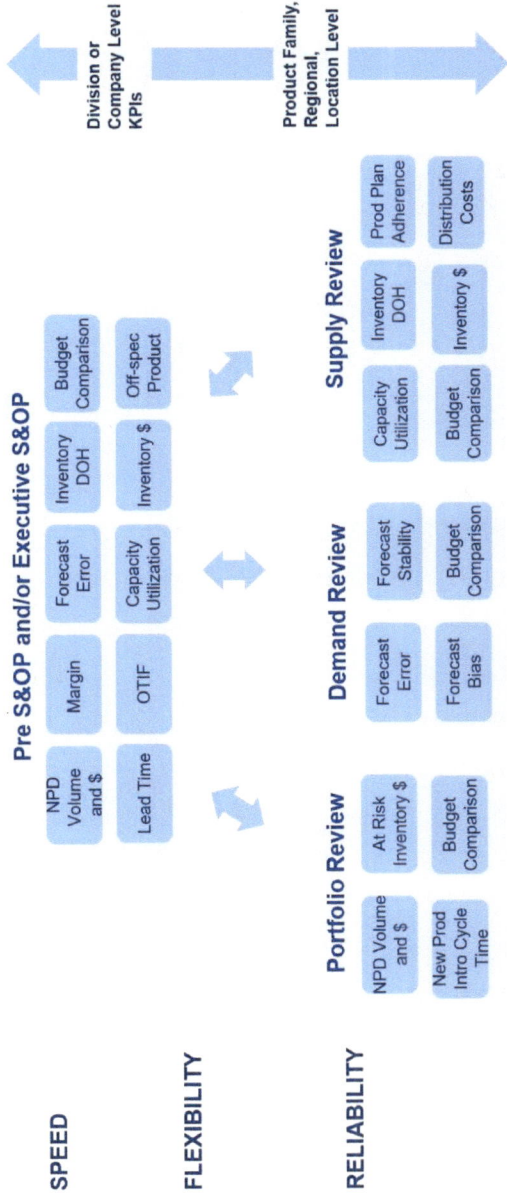

Division or Company Level KPIs

Product Family, Regional, Location Level

Pre S&OP and/or Executive S&OP

| NPD Volume and $ | Margin | Forecast Error | Inventory DOH | Budget Comparison |
| Lead Time | OTIF | Capacity Utilization | Inventory $ | Off-spec Product |

Portfolio Review

| NPD Volume and $ | At Risk Inventory $ |
| New Prod Intro Cycle Time | Budget Comparison |

Demand Review

| Forecast Error | Forecast Stability |
| Forecast Bias | Budget Comparison |

Supply Review

| Capacity Utilization | Inventory DOH | Prod Plan Adherence |
| Budget Comparison | Inventory $ | Distribution Costs |

SPEED

FLEXIBILITY

RELIABILITY

TOTAL COST

Results are necessary for success

Our experience and research show potential improvements are usually in the 10-20% range in the areas of:

- Forecast error
- Inventory turns
- On-time-in-full
- Lead times
- New product introduction
- Sales
- Margins
- Distribution costs
- Procurement costs
- Organization

Your results will of course vary with your starting point, and how diligent you are in tracking them and driving change.

Change needs active management

Change needs to be actively planned for and managed. It needs leaders and managers. We've had clients that say "everyone's on-board" and "we're doing this", which is good, but when it comes down to it, companies are overwhelmed in today's world, and this is one more thing to deal with. These projects are high visibility and have many moving parts with stakeholders of varying priorities and backgrounds.

Everything we've talked about thus far contributes to the change.

- The S&OP design needs to be integrated with organization structure
- The vision is used to communicate, educate, set expectations and common goals, manage scope, and evaluate success.
- You need a strong sponsor
- IT will be required
- An assessment aligns the team, sets expectations, and justifies resources and time
- The right reports matter and the meetings have other tools/techniques that go with them
- You need to demonstrate results

Change needs active management

Change management is about both "hard" and "soft" techniques.

CHANGE MANAGEMENT

Vision

Motivating Others ("WIIFM")

Making Others Successful

Coaching

Stakeholder Analysis

Communication

Leadership

PROJECT MANAGEMENT

Steering Team

Project Team

Project Plans

Milestones

Results Tracking

Status Reports/Meetings

Resources and Budgets

Structure and Task Execution

You need to hit change from many different angles, some of the items will be more effective than others in your particular situation. The point is all the items work together and skipping them is like removing blocks from the Jenga stack, remove too many or the wrong one, and the house comes down.

Do you need a consultant?

Hiring a consultant basically comes down to a question of your internal subject matter knowledge and your ability to get change and results within your organization.

Most consultants I've worked with are:

- Smart, hard-working, and get results for their clients
- Take their clients' challenges personally
- Good at listening to clients, eager to share knowledge, and want to learn too
- Quick to adapt to a new industry
- Adept at dealing with change management issues
- Under pressure to deliver results, we don't just float along from client to client
- Motivated. We have varying degrees of job security, but whether employees or independents, most of us don't know where our next project (i.e. livelihood) is coming from.

For clients, this enables consultants to:

- Give all they can, while they can
- Come with expertise from other situations, a methodology, and a plan
- Say what needs to be said, when it needs to be said, to whom it needs to be said
- Decrease the time to get to the end result

Do you need a consultant?

- Be there when you can't be (perhaps in another geography or where-ever)
- Share risk with clients when appropriate
- Get change in an interfacing part of the organization
- Be objective, but also echo and put a data-based story around what you perhaps already know to be true
- Act as task masters if your organization struggles with execution (as most do)

Certainly there are cons as well:

- Cost. Especially in non-ROI (i.e. benefits case) situations, the focus can go here.
- Organizational disruption. We ask for things (e.g. data, peoples' time, executive involvement).
- Pace (if too fast for your organization). We're on a budget (yours). We can flex, but when projects drag out it usually adds cost. Pace can also be a pro.
- Visibility. It's expensive, what if it still fails?
- Admitting you need help. Some leaders still struggle with this.

Thank you and download a gift

I hope this short guide has given you an idea of what S&OP is and what is involved. There's so much more to discuss, but that's not the intent of a primer. More content is also available on Nexview Online. I also have a full book on implementation and Nexview's performance improvement methodologies well in progress.

As a thank you, I'd like to offer you a simple, but effective tool we use with clients for free. It's our S&OP Meeting Effectiveness Scorecard. This is just a spreadsheet which means you can tailor it to specific S&OP meeting components and your individual needs. We use it with clients to improve behaviors and track progress over time as part of maturity tracking programs we implement with them.

Just go to the Nexview website at

http://bit.ly/nexview-jumpstart-booklink

to download the scorecard.

Thank you and download a gift

Review offer

If you'd like to post a review this booklet, I'd be happy to send you a comprehensive S&OP best practice benchmarking tool that we use with clients during assessments. We use it not only in the assessment, but also in the maturity journey in combination with the meeting scorecard and other items.

After reviewing this primer, just send an email to info@nexviewconsulting.com including a link to the review and we'll send you the benchmarking tool.

You can post your review here:

https://bit.ly/sop-jumpstart-review-paperback

Thanks for spending a little time here, please follow Nexview Consulting on LinkedIn, and best in your improvement efforts!

-EJT

About the author

Eric Tinker leads Nexview Consulting and has over 25 years in management consulting helping clients achieve large-scale change within their organizations. His projects have resulted in over $500 million in operational improvements. These results have been achieved through a combination of improving business processes, management systems and tools, information systems, organizational effectiveness, and by helping clients achieve sustainable behavioral change.

His client experience spans several countries and ranges from helping start-ups to leadership of large, complex, multi-geography business transformation. Eric focuses on Sales & Operations Planning as well as the underlying processes and infrastructure. He has taught and consulted across 5 continents, has published several articles, and is the author of *Sales & Operations Planning RESULTS*. His industry experience includes Consumer Goods, Energy, Chemicals, Life Sciences, and High Tech, among others.

Prior to founding Nexview Consulting, Eric worked for organizations such as Celerant Consulting, Deloitte & Touche, Plan4Demand, and Hughes Aircraft. He is a CPA and holds a B.S. in Aerospace Engineering from Syracuse University, an M.S. in Mechanical Engineering from California State University-Northridge, and an MBA from the University of Southern California.

In addition to helping clients be successful, Eric enjoys training, supporting, and speaking at industry events. He has spoken at Institute of Business Forecasting, IE Group, APICS, Institute for Supply Management, and other public events as well as numerous private events.

Please feel free to connect with Eric on LinkedIn and follow the Nexview company page.

See more on Nexview Online

nexview online

Multimedia archive

Blog Posts

Articles

eBooks

Benchmarking Surveys

Conference Presentations

Infographics

Videos

Tools & Templates

Some articles and books/eBooks that may help you

"Revitalize Your S&OP"
Journal of Business Forecasting

"Directing Success – 10 Tips for S&OP Sponsors"
APICS Magazine

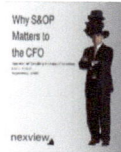

"Why S&OP Matters to the CFO"
Journal of
Trading Partner Practices

"26 Ways to Get Sales On Board with Demand Planning"
Supply Chain Quarterly

Sales & Operations Planning RESULTS
Full book on Amazon.com

S&OP Implementation Success
eBook pre-release of next full book on
our implementation methodology and tips

Choose the Right Supply Chain Consultant
eBook, An insider's candid perspective